TO KNOW ME IS TO LOVE ME

STEPS TO ENCOURAGE YOURSELF AND OTHERS

Lynn Lott
Marilyn Matulich Kentz
Dru West

Official manual for the certified training
Encouragement Consultant Training de Lynn Lott

Dedicated to our mothers and fathers
who taught us about courage.

With special thanks to Julio Velasco who helped make the revision possible and to Wendy Barton whose skill, kindness and smarts were invaluable in all the editing that took place and who helped make this book a useful tool for encouragement seekers everywhere.

Copyright © 2015. Lynn Lott, Marilyn Matulich Kentz and Dru West. All rights reserved.

No part of this publication may be reproduced, distributed, or transmitted in any form or by any means, including photocopying, recording, or other electronic or mechanical methods, without the prior written permission of the publisher, except in the case of brief quotations embodied in critical reviews and certain other non-commercial uses permitted by copyright law. For permission requests, write to lynnlott@sbcglobal.net.

ISBN 978-1-7340820-8-1 (paperback)
ISBN 978-1-7340820-9-8 (ebook)

Lynn Lott Encouragement Consulting
www.lynnlottec.com

FOREWORD

Jennifer remembers a time when her mother was too busy to spend time with her. She wondered if she was important to her mother. At the wise old age of four, she answered this question with "No, I'm not important." Even though she was not consciously aware of her decision, Jennifer proceeded through life trying to prove she was important. Since she had already decided she was not, she couldn't accept any evidence to the contrary. However, she was very willing to accept evidence to support her decision that she was not important.

As I explain to my own clients when I use an activity called "Trivia Question Therapy," understanding the questions that have presented themselves to us during our childhood years, and our answers to these questions, can help us understand ourselves. It is interesting that even though we are not consciously aware of the questions or the answers, we often base our lives on these answers.

When Jennifer relived the memory that led to her belief that she was not important, she used her "magic wand" to recreate a very different outcome and a new belief. She now knows that every time she feels that pit in her stomach she is reacting to the old belief. This becomes her signal to call up her new beliefs and skills, which are more appropriate today

To Know Me Is To Love Me includes many exercises and processes which help us become aware of some of the beliefs we adopted in childhood--beliefs that lead us away from our natural self esteem and create problems that hamper the joy of living. Once we become aware of how and why we created these beliefs, we can recreate new beliefs and skills that will serve us better and return us to our inherent sense ofself-esteem.

This book can be extremely useful to individuals who are willing to spend the time to carefully go through the suggested exercises. It can serve as a form of self-therapy or can be used in conjunction with more formal therapy.

The exercises and processes outlined in this book have been used by many therapists, groups and teachers who have found them to be effective and exciting tools to use with their clients and students to increase self-awareness and useful skills.

This is a "work" book for those who enjoy the exciting work of personal growth. I have personally experienced all of the exercises in this book and found them helpful and enlightening. Some of them have been used more than once for deeper awareness each time.

I highly recommend *To Know Me Is To Love Me* as an important investment in you. Give yourself time to go through the exercises and processes--by you, in a group, with a therapist or in a class. Enjoy the process of your own personal growth.

Jane Nelsen

TO KNOW ME IS TO LOVE ME

STEPS TO ENCOURAGE YOURSELF AND OTHERS

TABLE OF CONTENTS

FOREWORD		iii
INTRODUCTION	THE SEARCH FOR SELF-ESTEEM	1
CHAPTER 1	THE BEGINNING OF SELF-ESTEEM	9
CHAPTER 2	MESSAGES FROM THE PAST	14
CHAPTER 3	FEELING LOVED	18
CHAPTER 4	CIRCLE AWAY FROMSELF- ESTEEM	26
CHAPTER 5	WHEN SELF-ESTEEM IS THREATENED	30
CHAPTER 6	MEMORY MAPS: FINDING THE CHILD WITHIN	37
CHAPTER 7	HEALING SELF-ESTEEM	42
CHAPTER 8	FEELING WORDS	48
CHAPTER 9	USING FEELINGS EFFECTIVELY	49
CHAPTER 10	UNCOVERING ANGER	53
CHAPTER 11	THINK, FEEL, DO	59
CHAPTER 12	SETTING GOALS	63
CHAPTER 13	UNDERSTANDING	67

TO KNOW ME IS TO LOVE ME

STEPS TO ENCOURAGE YOURSELF AND OTHERS

INTRODUCTION

THE SEARCH FOR SELF-ESTEEM

The key ingredients in the journey to becoming an encouragement consultant are:

⭐ Courage to be imperfect

⭐ Courage to accept yourselves just as you are

⭐ Courage to take risks--to try new behaviors

⭐ Courage to let go

Anything that validates, accepts and acknowledges who you are in any given moment -- without judgments, comparisons, shoulds and have to's – raises self-esteem.

The activities in this book help with theses three areas

 **Awareness**   How to discover who you are and how you see yourself in this very moment.

 **Acceptance**   How to accept yourself by letting go of judgments, criticisms, comparisons, shoulds and have to's.

 **Action**   How to have courage to do homework in the real world by creating new options and learning from your mistakes.

Question: "Where does encouragement come from?"

Answer: "Encouragement comes from the decisions you made about what you saw happening around you and to you. You started making those decisions long before you ever had words or language."

Question: "Where was I when that happened?"

Answer: "Probably in your family"

Question: "How did my decisions about myself discourage me?"

Answer: "When you made the mistakes of thinking you were only good enough **IF OR WHEN** you behaved in a certain way so that others would love you, or when you made the decision that you weren't good enough, so why bother? This began when you started comparing yourself to others (to your parents, your siblings, your cousins, or to other people in the neighborhood) and believed that they were better, stronger, smarter, braver and more talented or more courageous than you.

It also began when you started thinking that when others were angry at you and when problems happened around you that it was your fault, or when you believed someone else's negative statements about you."

Discouragement

is a loss of courage.

A fear that you have to be careful

and do certain things or be a certain way

so people will love you. Discouragement is giving up,

deciding you've already lost love or respect

and that there's no way to get it back.

You need to get your courage back because

with courage a person can do anything!

It's the effort that counts,

the action,

the attempt,

the doing.

Nothing ventured, nothing gained.

Fear of making a mistake stops your action.

Courage lets you move and accept that mistakes

are part of being human.

It's not the mistake that's important, but what you learn

from it and what you do afterward that counts.

Are there no limits to what a person can do?

Not if what a person does is
respectful to himself and to others.

Remember... Anything that validates, accepts and acknowledges who you are in any given moment -- without judgments, comparisons, shoulds and have to's -- is encouragement.

When you feel encouraged, it's easier to have courage to go out and try out new behaviors and create new options in the real world.

In addition to awareness and acceptance, you need action. We call this doing your "homework" in the real world. The activities in this book are set up to help you accomplish this task.

Who owns courage?

Each individual.

And the more you know and accept yourself

for who you are

the greater the courage.

Use the 3A

Each activity in this book is set up so that at the end of each section you'll have an Encouragement Summary Worksheet that will show you:

Awareness — How you see yourself in the very moment. This summary statement begins with the words ***I'm a person who.***

Acceptance — How you can get rid of judgment and accept yourself in the very moment. This summary statement begins with the words ***Without judgment.***

Action — How you can use that self-acceptance to instill courage to do "homework" in the real world. This summary statement begins with the words ***With courage to do homework in the real world, a smallstep I can take is.***

Most of you, most of the time, did what was needed or necessary to meet the needs of the situations you were in, but sometimes you felt unsure, afraid, or worried that things wouldn't go your way or that you wouldn't be loved. You lost your courage because you started to believe you weren't good enough just the way you were. Your self-esteem was threatened. You felt inadequate, ashamed and guilty and thought you wouldn't measure up.

When you were kids you made another mistake.
You didn't realize that you were really good enough just as you were.
You didn't know that you didn't have to do anything special to be loved.

1. When you were born you were good enough just the way you were.

Good enough

2. At some point you thought you weren't good enough, which you believed to be a minus.

—

3. When that happened, without thinking, you started to overcompensate. That is, you tried to do something that you believed would prove you really were okay, something to get love. Your thinking was very black and white because you were small children at the time.

You decided things like:

4. All this trying to prove your worth took you farther away from the you that was you.

5. As you learn to be an encouragement consultant, you'll find ways back to the **X** ¡the place where you know you are good enough just the way you are!

CHAPTER 1

THE BEGINNING OF SELF-ESTEEM

The To find out how you first saw yourself, let's look at some of the decisions you made about yourself when you were just a little kid.

When you were a child you lived in a family. You often thought things were black or white. Sometimes you thought the family was like a pie, with just so many pieces to go around.
You might have thought that if one piece of the pie was taken, you had to take a different piece.

You made decisions about who you were by comparing yourself to your brothers and sisters. If you were an only child, you compared yourself to your parents, cousins or kids in the neighborhood. The conclusions you made about yourself as a child stayed with you your entire life.

You made decisions about who you were by comparing yourself to your brothers and sisters. If you were an only child, you compared yourself to your parents, cousins or kids in the neighborhood. The conclusions you made about yourself as a child stayed with you your entire life.

Fill in the blanks for your family pie.

Activity:

1. Write the names of all the kids in your family, including yourself, using one section of the pie for each person. Put the age difference (plus or minus) from your age for each child. Include the names of children who died. If you had more than one family (for example, a blended family, etc.) use the names of people who you think of as your family. Put a star beside your own name.

2. Write two or three words that describe each person when you were kids, including yourself.

3. Notice how you decided each person was different and special.

4. Notice what you decided about yourself.

5. Do you still feel that way today?

6. How does that decision affect your life?

The pieces of your family pie show how people in our own family learned overcompensation, or at least how you think you overcompensate. As a growing child, you had to sort out, organize and make sense out of so many things.

You were a good observer but your conclusions about what you observed weren't as good and you overcompensated.

When you look at the pie today through your adult eyes, you can remind yourself that you are more complex that those black and white pictures from your childhood.

You can also think about whether you are doing things to keep yourself in the same spot in the pie today.

SELF - ESTEEM SUMMARY WORKSHEET

In this activity I learned:

Awareness   I'm a person who is _____
_____
_____
_____
_____
(Fill in with the adjectives you used to describe yourself in your family.)

Acceptance   Do you hear an inner voice? Is it arguing? Judging? Explaining? Defending? Protecting? Comparing? Limiting? Which?_____

To accept yourself, pick a statement below that fits for you, or create your own.

1. It's okay to be different from my siblings. Differences make the world more interesting.
2. Isn't that interesting that I still see myself that way.
3. I notice I have a hard time accepting some of these qualities.
4. Just because I wrote a quality for a sibling doesn't mean it doesn't apply to me.
5. I don't have to limit my view of myself to just these qualities.
6. I accept myself in spite of my faults and imperfections.
7. _____

 **Action** With courage to do homework in the real world, pick one small step you could take from the list below now that you have that information about yourself. (Just pick one for now. You can always do more later.)

1. Share the adjectives you wrote down for yourself with someone else and ask them to repeat them back to you.

2. Practice saying, "I am (your adjectives)" to see where it leads.

3. Look for ways those adjectives limit you now.

4. Give yourself permission to be just who you are.

5. Find the quality you think only your sibling has and tell how you have it too.

6. Notice if you have a very negative or limited description for one of your siblings and find some ways to expand your knowledge of that person.

7. Look at whom you are comparing yourself to and why. Let it go!

CHAPTER 2

MESSAGES FROM THE PAST

Based on a workshop by Maxine Ijams

The conclusions you came to as a child are often the same ideas you have about life today. You operate in an adult body, in your adult world, using your childhood reasoning.

You carry these conclusions and old messages as baggage. What is some of your baggage?

To find out, fill in the blanks in the suitcases with whatever comes to your mind when you look at the following words or think of the messages you got as a child about each of these categories.

Activity:
(Fill in the blanks.)

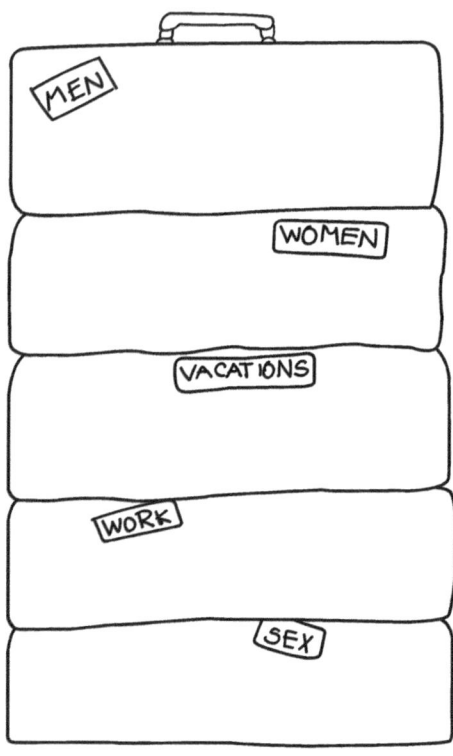

The messages you got as a child become beliefs you hold as an adult

SELF - ESTEEM SUMMARY WORKSHEET

In this activity I learned:

Awareness

I'm a person who is believes _____
_____
_____
_____
(Fill in one of your old messages or conclusions form one of the suitcases.)

Acceptance

Without Judgment. Pick the statement that fits for you or create your own.

1. It's okay that my baggage is different from someone else's.
2. Isn't that interesting that this came up for me.
3. Isn't it interesting that this old thinking is still with me?
4. I've been noticing how that thinking has been limiting me.
5. I had no idea this was something I created as a child and it's a surprise to know where that came from.
6. _____

Action

With courage to do homework in the real world, ask yourself whether your belief is creating mischief for you or not. MISCHIEF is doing any more or any less than what needs to be done.

If yes, state how: _____
_____
_____
_____

IF IT IS, then think of a small step you could take to use this information to enrich your current situation. Some steps might be:

1. To share your belief with someone else.
2. Listen to other people's beliefs and see if you want to borrow their attitudes.
3. Listen to other people's beliefs and do the opposite.
4. Make an action plan of one thing you could do in the next week to improve on your situation.

My step will be:
_____
_____
_____
_____
_____

IF YOUR BELIEF IS NOT MAKING MISCHIEF, then your homework in the real world could be to write down how the belief has helped you grow. Write it down.

This belief has helped me _____
_____
_____
_____
_____
_____
_____
_____

A Note: Sometimes this baggage can get you in trouble, especially in relationships. You might think others see the world just as you do, but they carry different baggage. When different baggage collides and both of you think your way is the right way, it's time to develop an attitude of curiosity instead of fighting to be right and ending up in a power struggle. You can practice by doing this activity with a friend or partner and then sharing your answers with each other.

CHAPTER 3

FEELING LOVED

This activity was first introduced by Gloria Lane

The family is the first place you learn about love. Most of what you learned happened at such an early age that you don't usually think about what you learned or how you learned it.

Your parents treated you in ways in which you experienced feeling loved, and you discovered ways to show your parents that you cared about them. These early experiences shape the way you feel and show love today. What makes each of you feel loved varies from person to person because of the differences in those early experiences and what you decided about them.

The ways in which you and others show love is just as varied.

To understand your early decisions about love, fill in the following blanks. (There is a duplicate set of questions for your partner to use if you'd like to do this activity with him or her.)

YOU

1. Who do you think was your primary parent or adult mentor from birth to one year?
   _____

2. Who was your favorite parent or adult mentor when you were a kid growing up?
   _____

3. As a child growing up, how did you show your primary parent or adult mentor (#1) you loved him/her?
   _____
   _____
   _____
   _____

5. As a child growing up, how did you show your favorite parent or adult mentor (#2) that you loved him/her? (Fill in only if you had a favorite parent/mentor.)

_____
_____
_____
_____
_____
_____
_____
_____
_____

6. How did your favorite parent or adult mentor (#2) show you that he/she loved you when you were growing up?

_____
_____
_____
_____
_____
_____
_____
_____
_____
_____
_____

(If you use words such as "Be good," "Be responsible," etc., try to define what that means more clearly. For example, "Be good," might really mean "Do chores on time" or "Be quiet" or "Do what I was asked.")

YOUR PARTNER

1. Who do you think was your primary parent or adult mentor from birth to one year?
_____

2. Who was your favorite parent or adult mentor when you were a kid growing up?
_____

3. As a child growing up, how did you show your primary parent or adult mentor (#1) you loved him/her?
_____
_____
_____
_____
_____

5. As a child growing up, how did you show your favorite parent or adult mentor (#2) that you loved him/her? (Fill in only if you had a favorite parent/mentor.)
_____
_____
_____
_____
_____
_____
_____
_____

6. How did your favorite parent or adult mentor (#2) show you that he/she loved you when you were growing up?
_____
_____
_____
_____
_____
_____
_____
_____

(If you use words such as "Be good," "Be responsible," etc., try to define what that means more clearly. For example, "Be good," might really mean "Do chores on time" or "Be quiet" or "Do what I was asked.")

If you do this activity with your partner, see if the way you show love matches up with the way your partner feels loved. If it doesn't, that's not unusual but it's useful information to help you understand your relationship.

What does this information mean? Let's say you just completed the questions and you discovered you show love by

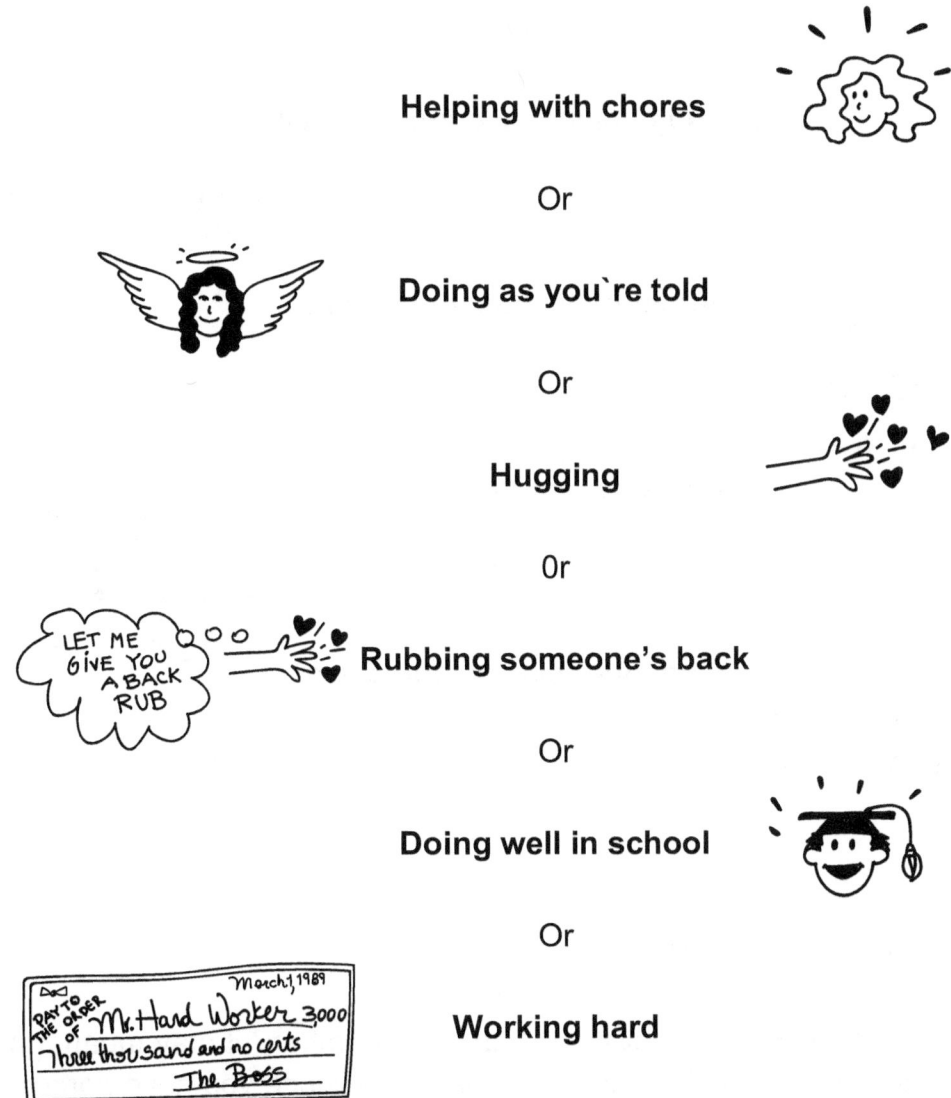

Perhaps you do these things and people around you complain because they don't feel loved. You feel hurt, angry, confused. How could that be?

Maybe if you looked at their answers you'd discover they feel loved when

 **Someone is playful with them**

Or

Someone cooks a nice meal each night

Or

Someone leaves them alone

 Or

Someone lets them be on top

Or

Someone relaxes with them.

Consider some of the possibilities for your life.

If you answered, "I didn't show or feel love," or "I don't remember," it may mean that you don't notice when someone was showing love or it may mean that since you have nomodel, you can be open to learning ways to show love.

Now take the answers you gave to the questions and transfer them into the corresponding boxes to find out your current model for showing and feeling love. There's room here for you to include answers from your partner.

22

Feeling Loved Chart

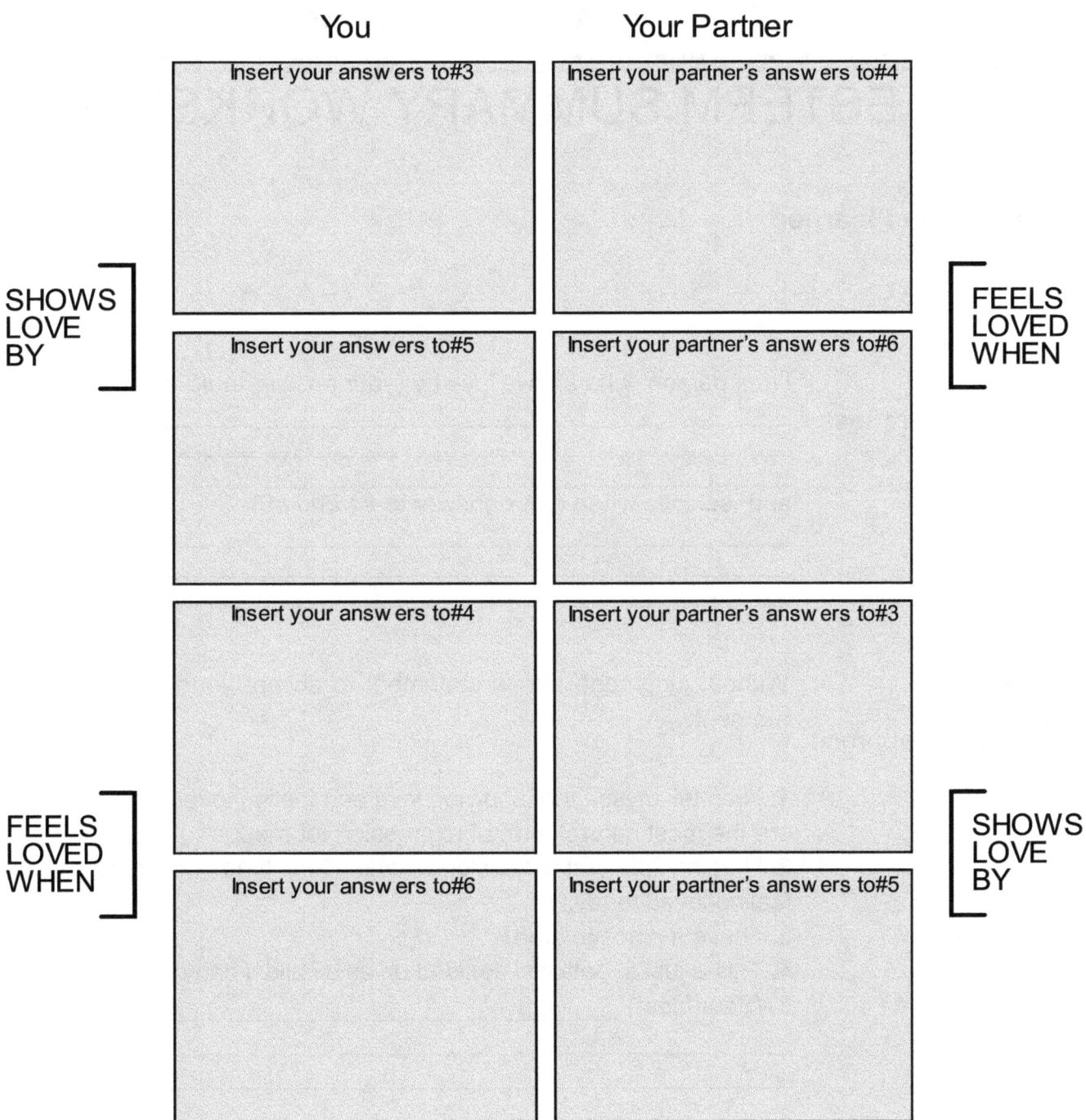

23

SELF - ESTEEM SUMMARY WORKSHEET

In this activity I learned:

Awareness   I'm a person who shows love by (your answer to #3 and #5)
_____
_____

and feel love when (your answer to #4 and #6)
_____
_____
_____

Acceptance   Without judgment, pick a statement to accept yourself in the very moment.

1. I can tell myself that showing love and feeling loved in these ways are the most natural form of expression for me.
2. I had no idea that a decision I made a long time ago affects my not feeling loved today.
3. I have a place to start.
4. This is just a. pattern I decided on as a child. I can change it if I like.
5. (Your idea!) _____
_____
_____
_____
_____

 **Action**   With courage to do homework in the real world, pick one of the items below:

1. Look at the areas where you feel unloved or wish someone were showing you love. See if you're waiting for them to do what your parents used to do or what you used to do instead of noticing that they may be showing you love in their own way.

2. Ask someone for love in the way you feel most loved. You may believe that if you have to ask for something, it's not as good. Remember that other people aren't mind readers. They need to learn what makes you feel loved. If you ask and they don't give, it doesn't mean you're not lovable. How they respond is about their ability to respond, not about you.

3. Take time to look for ways people who are important to you are really showing you love.

4. Ask someone if the way you show love makes them feel loved. Ask if there were something else they would like.

5. When you show someone you love them by doing the same things you learned as a child (Your answers to #3 and #5), tell them "I'm doing this because I love you. This is the way I show love."

6. To deal with any pain you have about feeling unloved, try talking to someone about your feelings.

7. Behave "as if" you're loved and loving.

8. Have your partner answer the questions in this activity so you can learn more about him or her.

9. Create an affirmation for yourself that says, "I feel good the way it is. It's nice to have this information about myself and to understand what I do."
Sometimes you'd like to make a change, but you get yourself into a ...

CHAPTER 4

CIRCLE AWAY FROM SELF-ESTEEM

Thanks again to Gloria Lane
The The circle away from self-esteem is a rut you create in your mind. It's similar to being in a treadmill like a hamster. You think there's no way out.

Here's what a circle away from self-esteem looks like.
Follow the numbers...

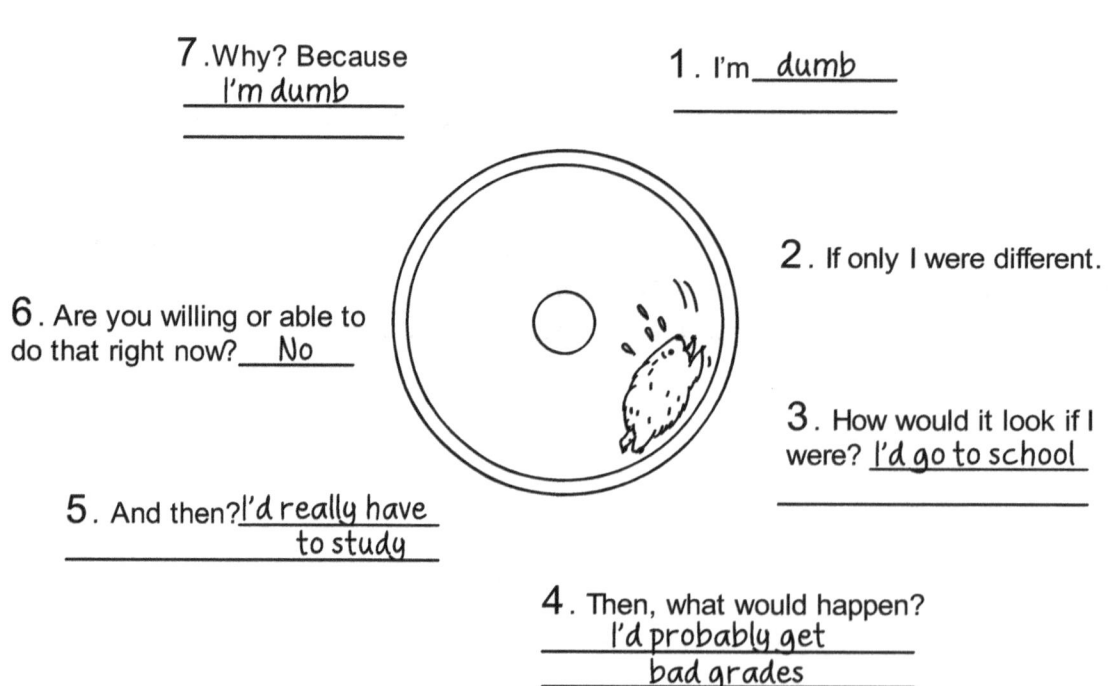

7. Why? Because __I'm dumb__

1. I'm __dumb__

2. If only I were different.

6. Are you willing or able to do that right now? __No__

3. How would it look if I were? __I'd go to school__

5. And then? __I'd really have to study__

4. Then, what would happen? __I'd probably get bad grades__

26

Activity:

Now do yours. Write down something you'd like to change about yourself. It could be something you don't like about yourself or something you wish were different.

Here's what a circle away from self-esteem looks like.
Follow the numbers...

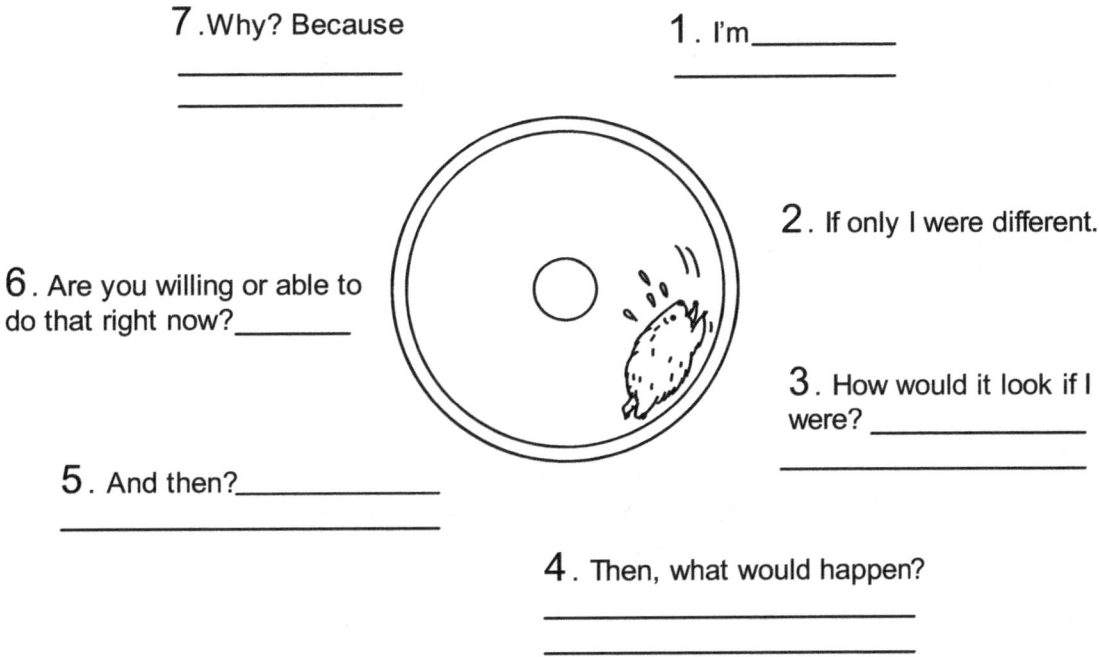

7. Why? Because _____
  _____

1. I'm _____
  _____

6. Are you willing or able to do that right now? _____

2. If only I were different.

3. How would it look if I were? _____
  _____

5. And then? _____
  _____

4. Then, what would happen?
  _____
  _____

When you play out your circle away from self-esteem, notice what you get. Is this what you want? If not, go back to your circle to see how you might be discouraging yourself with any of the following discouraging behaviors:

 Comparing yourself

⭐ Judging yourself

⭐ Listening to what others say and believing their statements are about you but not them

⭐ Expecting too much

⭐ Thinking in absolutes, i.e., always, never, can't

⭐ Believing you could never change and that your old patterns are your ONLY patterns

To ENCOURAGE yourself substitute one of the following new behaviors in Steps #3 and #4 of the circle:

IF	THEN
COMPARING	Focus on your own progress, accept differences, and learn skills.
JUDGING OR THINKING IN ABSOLUTES	Change your: "shoulds," "have to's," and "musts" to "coulds" "might," "can," or "will." Change: "always" to "sometimes," "never" to "perhaps," "can't" to "don't want to."
LISTENING TO OTHERS' PICTURES	Remind yourself that what others say is a statement about them, not about you.
EXPECTING TOO MUCH OR BELIEVING YOU COULD NEVER CHANGE	A. Think of one small step you could take or focus on one day at a time. B. Have a little FAITH in yourself! C. Spend time with people who are there to encourage you, such as Weight Watchers, a Women's Support Group or other support groups. D. Ask yourself what you're afraid of losing or how your life would be different if you gave up this problem.

SELF - ESTEEM SUMMARY WORKSHEET

In this activity I learned:

Awareness

I'm a person who thinks I'm
_____
_____
(Fill in #1 from your circle)

Acceptance

Without judgment, I have a tendency for _____
_____
_____

(Look at your circle and see if you are doing any of the following. Write in which of these you do.)

Comparing
Judging
Thinking in absolutes
Listening to others' pictures
Expecting too much
Believing I can't

After filling in the blanks, tell yourself "That's okay; that's just what I do."

Action

With courage to do homework in the real world, choose from the "Then" column on Page 28.

I can_____
_____
_____

CHAPTER 5

WHEN SELF-ESTEEM IS THREATENED

Based on a workshop by Bill and Mim Pew

As long as things go your way and you don't feel threatened, you do just fine. You coast or meet life's tasks, but when you feel threatened you've learned a way to respond that you think will protect you, save your ego, or get you off the hook.

You can do this response on automatic pilot without giving it a thought. This response is a style of behavior you use to deal with situations that threaten your sense of self. It's called your Top Card.

The following activity will help you find your Top Card. Once you're aware of what it is, you can notice when you play it and what happens to you when you do.

Circle the box that has the things inside that you would most want to avoid.

If it's hard for you to decide which box you'd circle, imagine yourself having to open three of the boxes but being able to hide one box under the bed and never having to open it.

If you Chose:	Your Top Card is:	And What You Do Is:
 STRESS AND PAIN	COMFORT 	Take the path of least resistance, leave sentences incomplete, make jokes, intellectualize, do only the things you already do well, avoid new experiences, do anything you can to keep people from finding out you made a mistake, don't take risks if you might hurt someone's feelings, hide and avoid.
 REJECTION AND HASSLES	PLEASING 	Act friendly, gossip instead of confronting directly, say "yes" when you mean "no," give in, worry about what others want more than about your own needs, try to fix everything and make everybody happy.
 CRITICISM AND RIDICULE	CONTROL 	Do it yourself, hold back, boss others, organize, argue, get quiet and wait for others to coax you, stuff your feelings, cover all the bases before you make a move and procrastinate.
 MEANINGLESSNESS AND UNIMPORTANCE	SUPERIORITY 	Put down people or things, correct others, knock yourself, talk about the absurdity of life, over-do, take on too much, worry about always doing better, and operate on "shoulds."

WHAT YOU GET WHEN YOU PLAY YOUR TOP CARD

When you play your top card, it can take you to a positive place or it can take you to problems.

Top Card:	Positives:	Problems:
COMFORT 	Look out for self and own needs, can count on others to help, make others feel comfortable, creative.	Invite special service and attention, worry a lot but no one knows how scared you are, lose out on the contact of sharing, juggle uncomfortable situations rather than confront them, wait to be taken care of instead of becoming independent.
PLEASING 	Have lots of friends, people count on you, you can usually see the positives in things and people.	Invite revenge cycles, feel resentful and ignored, get in trouble for trying to look good while being bad.
CONTROL 	Organized, get what you want, able to get things done and figure things out, take charge of situations, wait patiently	End up not being close to people, invite power struggles, end up sick, and avoid dealing with issues when you feel criticized and get defensive instead of open, sometimes wait for permission.
SUPERIORITY 	Make people laugh, get a lot done and receive a lot of praise, awards or prizes, don't have to wait for other people to tell you what to do to get things done, have a lot of selfconfidence.	Seen as a know-it-all or a rude and insulting person and don't know it's a problem, never happy because you could have done more or better, have to put up with so many imperfect people around you, sometimes you don't do anything because it seems too overwhelming.

IF YOU WOULD LIKE TO BE A FRIEND TO SOMEONE WHOSE TOP CARD IS:

COMFORT

THEN YOU...

Don't interrupt, invite their comments, listen quietly, leave room for them, show faith, don't do for them, encourage them to take small steps.

PLEASING

THEN YOU...

Tell them how much you love them, touch them a lot, show approval, tell them how much you appreciate what they do, tell them how special they are.

CONTROL

THEN YOU...

Ask how they feel, tell them the rules, ask for their help, say "Okay," give choices, let them lead in the area they want to, give permission, ask advice, tell them you love them.

SUPERIORITY

THEN YOU...

Tell them how significant they are, thank them for their contributions, help them see the small steps, have fun with them.

SELF - ESTEEM SUMMARY WORKSHEET

In this activity I learned:

Awareness

I'm a person who automatically moves into
_____
_____
_____
(Fill in #1 from your Top Card.)

Acceptance

Without judgment, I can tell myself that I learned an automatic response of _____
_____
_____
_____
_____

Action

With courage to do homework in the real world, pick an activity from the following list:

Activity 1: Notice how others play their Top Card. Remind yourself that they're probably feeling afraid or stressed when they play their card. Write down what you noticed _____
_____
_____
_____

Activity 2: Notice yourself in a situation where you are playing your Top Card (see column three, page 33, for examples of what you might do.) When you catch yourself playing your card, say to yourself "Isn't it interesting I'm playing my Top Card." Write down the incident
_____
_____
_____
_____
_____

Activity 3 If you can catch yourself playing your Top Card, ask yourself, "What am I afraid of?" or "What's the worse thing that could happen and could I handle that?" (Use the incident from Activity 2.) I was afraid of _____

_____
_____
_____
_____
_____
_____

Activity 4 If you can get in touch with your fear, can you see another option or do you want to continue with your Top Card behavior? Write out what you want to do_____

_____
_____
_____
_____
_____
_____

Activity 5 Fill in the blanks

A. Think of a time when things weren't going the way you wanted then to. Write it down.

_____
_____
_____
_____
_____
_____

B. What's your Top Card? _____

D. What was your fear? _____

_____
_____
_____
_____
_____

E. What other options do you have? _____

_____
_____
_____
_____
_____
_____

CHAPTER 6

MEMORY MAPS: FINDING THE CHILD WITHIN

Many of the patterns you have as adults were first formed in childhood. Inside each of you, a child still exists and is often the part of you that is calling the shots. This activity is designed to meet that child within and to get to know him or her better.

1. Think of one time when you were young when you felt loss, pain or disappointment. Write out the situation in BOX #1; include your age at the time.

2. How did you feel at the time? (Use Feeling Words on page 48.) Write the feeling(s) in BOX #2.

3. At that time you made a decision that you may or may not have been aware of. What did you decide at that time? Write your decision in the THOUGHT SHAPE #3. (A decision usually sounds like this: "I'll wait them out," "I'll fight and scream until I get my way," "They don't take me seriously," or "No one listens to me," etc.)

4. Now write down what you did in BOX #4. (This is the action you did at the time.)

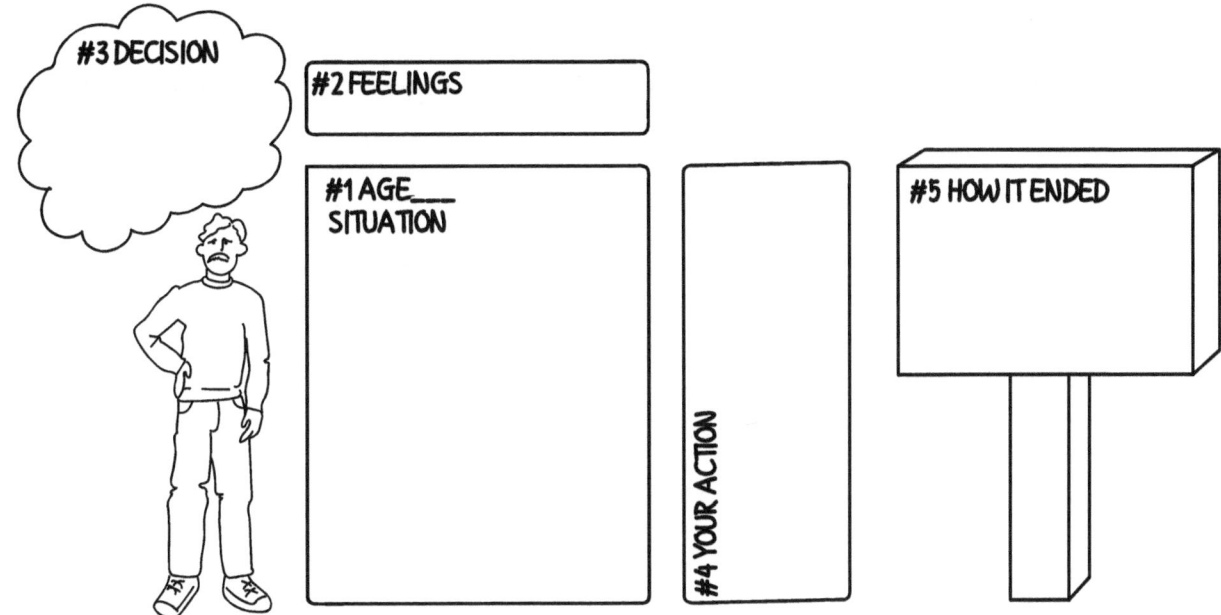

What situations invite the child within you to take over? To find out, look in BOX #1.

Often the information in BOX #1 stands for something. For instance, in the following example, the information about the pet cat stands for a time when the person didn't think she was being taken seriously and felt she was being put off.

When you look at this example further, you'll begin to see how the child within put the pieces of the experience together to make a decision about situations in which she doesn't think she's taken seriously or when she believes others are more important. In this example, the child within decided that when she's not being taken seriously (#1) and thinks others are more important (#3), she feels hysterical (#2), and believes she needs to scream to get attention (#4), and that is the only way she can get what she wants (#5).

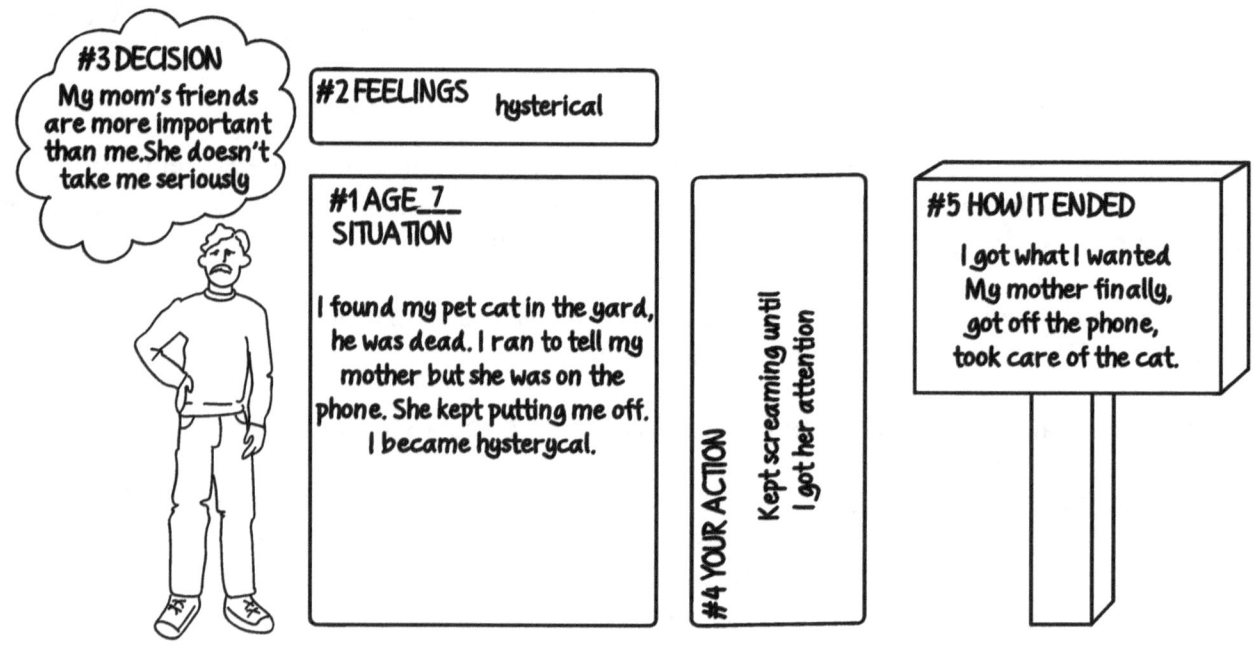

If this situation happened to you and your own child you might see the pattern quite clearly.

The childlike patterns formed when you were children may still be operating in situations you experience today as adults. Most of you recreate these patterns over and over again. This childhood memory map is a condensed version of how you learned to operate in the world and it shows how you think and feel, even today.

Looking at a current situation for the person in our previous example, we see a similar pattern.

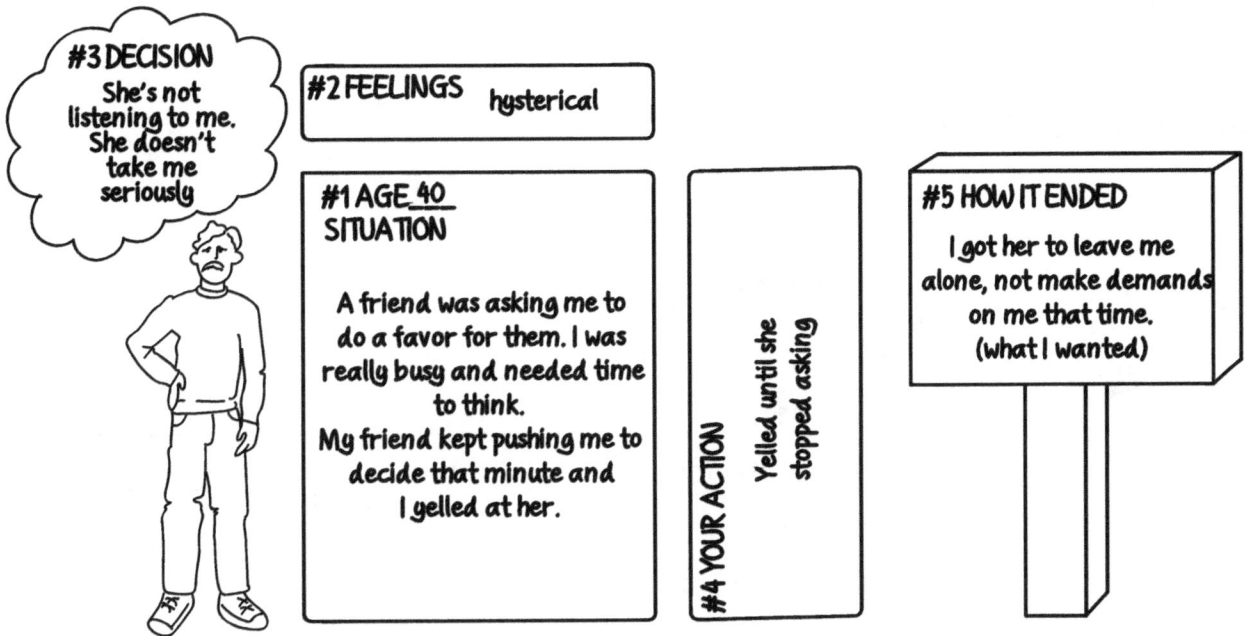

Having this map can very helpful in getting your power back because once you know that you created the pattern by yourself -- that it wasn't created by the people around you -- you can create another pattern, an optional pattern if you'd like.

SELF - ESTEEM SUMMARY WORKSHEET

In this activity I learned:

I'm a person who:

Think (#3) _____

When (#1) _____

Happens and feels (#2) _____

And Does (#4) _____

And ends up (#5) _____

_____

Without judgment, I can tell myself one of the following (pick one):

A. It's okay not to fix this or change it. It's just nice to know more about the child within me.

B. I can tell myself I can change this when I'm ready, if I want to.

C. Knowing about this is the first step in changing this.

 **A**ction

With courage to do homework in the real world, I can do one of the following activities. (Pick one you'd like to do.)

Activity 1: Be aware of your pattern.

Activity 2: Change your pattern by pretending you have a magic wand and picture the situation in #1 again the way you wish it had been. If you find yourself wanting to use your magic wand to change another person, think about what you could have done to bring about this change.

Activity 3: Talk about your child within to your partner or good friend.

Activity 4: Make friends with your child within and forgive him/her or ask the adult in you to give an encouraging message to the child within.

Activity 5: Look at a current situation and see you are still doing the old pattern. (Fill in the map below.)

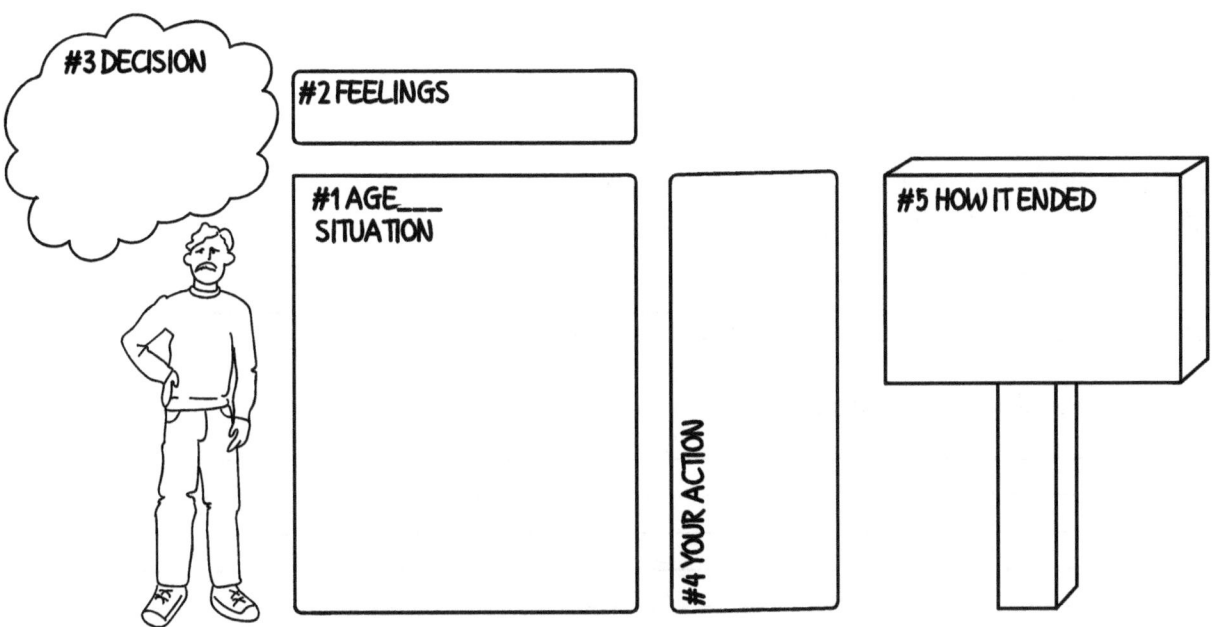

CHAPTER 7

HEALING SELF-ESTEEM

Based on the book Dealing with Feelings by Ed and Barbara Janoe

Do you sometimes get a feeling that is giving you a hard time? It might be pain, hunger, jealousy, stress, anger or any of a hundred others. You can reduce the pressure of the feeling or learn more about it by doing this activity. Use your imagination, let yourself exaggerate or pretend if necessary.

Activity:

Think of a feeling you would like some help with.
1. What is the name of the feeling?
_____
_____

(See page 48 for Feeling Words to help you name the feeling.)

2. Where is it located in your body?
_____
_____
_____
_____
_____

3. What does it look like in your body? (At this point you may need to pretend you can see the feeling.)
_____
_____
_____
_____
_____

4. What color is it?

5. What size is it?

6. What is the density?

7. How intense is it? (From 1 to 10, with 10 high.)

8. Think of a recent time you had the feeling and stop the action on that time. Describe it.

9. If you had a magic wand and could change anything you wanted in that last scene, how would you change it?

10. Go back as early as you can in your life and think of an early memory. It may or may not have the same feeling in it. If nothing comes to mind, any past scene will do. Stop the action. Describe it. (Be specific and think of one time in particular.)

        I remember one time when I was about ___ years old and

11. Again, how would you change that scene with a magic wand? (You may not want to change a thing and that's fine too.)

_____
_____
_____
_____
_____
_____

12. Now look at the feeling again.

What size is it?

_____
_____

What is the density?

_____
_____

How intense?

_____
_____

Has anything changed?

_____
_____

Usually the feeling you started with will be less intense by now or it may be gone. Sometimes another, stronger feeling will pop up. If so, just go through the same activity again.

This activity is a form of self-hypnosis. It can be used to reduce pain. It can be used to assist in reducing addictive behavior, and it can be used as a relaxation activity.

You can also learn about yourself and how you go about making changes. Sometimes awareness of this information is enough, or it can be the first step to making changes in your life and advancing your personal growth.

One way you can learn about yourself is to understand how you use the magic wand in the activity.

The magic wand symbolizes how you make changes. You can see how this works in your own life by going back to either the early memory or a current life situation in the preceding activity.

You're asked to use both of these because the feelings you have now come from decisions you made long ago but may not realize you made. Going back in time gives you a clearer view of your original decision and helps heal some of the pain from that earlier time.

SELF - ESTEEM SUMMARY WORKSHEET

In this activity I learned:

Awareness — I'm a person who sometimesfeels
_____
_____
_____
(Write in the feeling you worked on in thisactivity.)

Acceptance — Without judgment, I can tell myself "It's okay to feel that way. That`s just part of who I am."

Action — With courage to do homework in the real world, now that I have this information about myself:

1. My first step to use it for my personal growth could be to:
_____
_____
_____
_____
_____
_____
_____
_____
_____
_____
_____
_____
_____

2. Notice how you used the magic wand in either the early memory or current life situation. How could create that change in yourself now?

_____
_____
_____
_____
_____
_____
_____
_____
_____
_____
_____
_____
_____
_____

3. If you used your magic wand to change someone else, what could you do to invite that other person to behave that way now or to create the change you made with the magic wand?

_____
_____
_____
_____
_____
_____
_____
_____
_____
_____
_____
_____
_____
_____

CHAPTER 8

FEELING WORDS

CHAPTER 9

USING FEELINGS EFFECTIVELY

Whatever you feel tells you a lot about yourself. Feelings aren't right or wrong - they just are. Feelings are energy and this energy moves you in certain directions. However, sometimes your feelings move you away from what you really want.

This activity will help you get in touch with your feelings so you can learn how they help you or stop you from achieving your goals.

Let's see how this works.

Activity:

1. List three feelings you have today

A._____

B._____

C._____

2. How would you like to feel?

A._____

B._____

C._____

3. What do you usually do when you feel the feelings in #1 A, B and C?

Feeling 1 A: _____

Feeling 1 B: _____

Feeling 1 C: _____

4. Does this get you the feelings you'd like to have in #2 A, B and C? (Yes or No)

In 2 A? _____

In 2 B? _____

In 2 C? _____

5. If your answers to #3 don't get you the feelings you want in #2, can you think of some other actions you could take?

New 2 A:
_____
_____
_____
_____

New 2 B:
_____
_____
_____
_____

New 2 C:
_____
_____
_____
_____

6. If you're feeling stuck and can't think of other things to do, the following may help you create some new options.

a. Talk with someone else and ask them for their ideas or just share your feelings with them.

b. Remember a time when you felt the feelings in #2. What were you doing at that time? Could you do any of those now to get the feelings back?

c. Ask yourself, "If I had a magic wand, what would I do to get those feelings?"

What would it be?
_____
_____
_____
_____
_____
_____
_____
_____
_____
_____
_____
_____

(Sometimes using a magic wand in this way can get you unstuck and you may see new options.)

d. What would you tell a friend if they were looking for new options? Pretend you are the friend and tell it to
yourself._____
_____
_____
_____
_____
_____
_____
_____
_____
_____
_____

SELF - ESTEEM SUMMARY WORKSHEET

In this activity I learned:

Awareness — I'm a person who
_____
_____
_____
(Write in the feeling you worked on in this activity.)

Acceptance — Without judgment, I can say to myself "Feelings are just feelings and they take me in a direction. I'm learning what directions my feelings take me and it's okay to have these feelings today. That's just what I feel."

Action — With courage to do homework in the real world, I can do other things such as ... (Select from #5 or #6 in this activity.)

_____
_____
_____
_____
_____
_____
_____
_____
_____
_____
_____
_____

CHAPTER 10

UNCOVERING ANGER

Adapted from work by Mitch Messer

The feeling that is the hardest to admit to is usually anger because as children you were trained that it's not okay to be angry. When you were around angry people as children it was dangerous. As a child, you were usually sent to your room when you were angry or your parents became angrier with you for your own anger. Most of you learned that anger is something to hide, even when you still feel angry.

What many of you do, even as adults, is save up your anger and then explode. Then it IS a dangerous feeling to be around.

Feeling encouraged depends on noticing what you feel and giving the feeling the correct name. Anger is just one of the many feelings you are capable of experiencing.

Let's look at your anger.

Activity:

Think of something you're angry about. What is it?

A._____
_____
_____
_____
_____
_____
_____

Remember we said that anger is just a feeling. Feelings are inside of you. Sometimes when you're angry you think it outside of you. That is, you believe that someone or something caused it. Anger isn't caused. It's a response. In order to deal with the feeling it helps to understand what the feeling is directed at. The following list includes the five most common "objects of anger" -- the thing your anger is directed at. Can you find the object of your anger on this list?

B. Is this anger at?

Yourself?

Others?

Other people's anger at you?

Life?

An absent other?
(Someone who has died, moved away or is chemically dependent)

When you are angry you notice the feelings but you often don't realize that before you felt the feeling you had some thoughts going on inside of you.

Every person who's feeling angry has some underlying issue, or thoughts. To find your underlying issue you'll need to keep asking yourself, "What about that makes me angry?" until you find the real issue buried under a lot of other reasons. You'll find the real issue when you keep asking yourself this question and you find yourself coming back to the same answer. That's your underlying issue. Try it by using the example you started with.

C. What about that makes you angry?

_____
_____
_____
_____
_____
_____

And what about that makes you angry?

_____
_____
_____
_____
_____
_____

And what about that makes you angry?

_____
_____
_____
_____
_____
_____

And what about that makes you angry?

_____
_____
_____
_____
_____
_____
_____
_____

And what about that makes you angry?

_____
_____
_____
_____
_____
_____

And what about that makes you angry?

_____
_____
_____
_____
_____
_____

D. Now ask yourself whether your underlying issues are a statement about:

Recognition?
Power?
Justice?
Skills?

Recognition issues have to do with thoughts such as "What do people think about me?" "Am I being noticed?" "Do I deserve special treatment or service?" "What kind of person am I?"

Power issues have to do with thoughts such as "Nobody can do this to me." "I should be the boss." "I want it my way." "I feel powerless and helpless."

Justice issues have to do with thoughts such as "It's unfair." "Life is unfair." "It's not right to treat people that way." "People shouldn't treat people that way." "People should or shouldn't do certain things." "I wouldn't do that." "They're mean and hurtful."

Skills issues have to do with thoughts such as "I can`t do it." "It's not perfect." "It's never good enough." "I don't know how." "This is too hard." "I don't want to try."

What are your underlying issues about?

_____
_____
_____
_____
_____
_____
_____

SELF - ESTEEM SUMMARY WORKSHEET

In this activity I learned:

Awareness I'm a person who feels angry at
_____
_____
_____
_____

Acceptance Without judgment, I can tell myself that my anger is about issues of
_____
_____
_____

(Fill in with your underlying issues from #D.)

Action With courage to do homework in the real world, choose one from the following list below:

I'll _____
_____
_____
_____
_____

If object was:	Then I could:
SELF	Accept that imperfection is part of being human and that mistakes are opportunities to learn.
OTHERS	Tell the other "I'm angry at you because (use the information you learned) and I just want to let you know my feelings. It's fine not to fix this." (THEN have a little faith in the process.)
OTHER PEOPLE'S ANGER AT YOU	Ask the other person to tell you more about why he/she is angry and remind yourself that their anger is a statement about them, not about you.
LIFE	Write in a journal about your hurt feelings or share them with others. Often there is a lot of fear under this anger. Think about what your fears may be and share that too.
ABSENT OTHER	Write an angry letter or talk to an empty chair as if the person were there, telling him/her all about your anger. Or use a magic wand to recreate situations you are angry about but give it a different outcome in your imagination. Attend Alanon if AbsentOther is chemically dependent.

CHAPTER 11

THINK, FEEL, DO

What you *think* about problems has a tremendous effect upon what you feel and what you do to handle all the different areas in your life. This activity can help you discover how you can turn a destructive pattern into a constructive pattern

Activity:

Pick a situation in your life that is not satisfying, one you would like to change.

My situation is
_____
_____
_____
_____
_____

If you can, decide what your goal is for this situation. Write it down.

My goal is
_____
_____
_____
_____

Now answer the following questions:

1. What message do you give yourself --what you THINK -- about this situation?
_____
_____
_____
_____

(Transfer this information to the THINK circle.)

2. How do you FEEL when you think about this situation (Use the Feeling Faces in this book if you need help with feeling words.)
_____
_____
_____

(Transfer this information to the FEEL circle.)

3. What do you DO when you feel that way?
_____
_____
_____

(Transfer this information to the DO circle.)

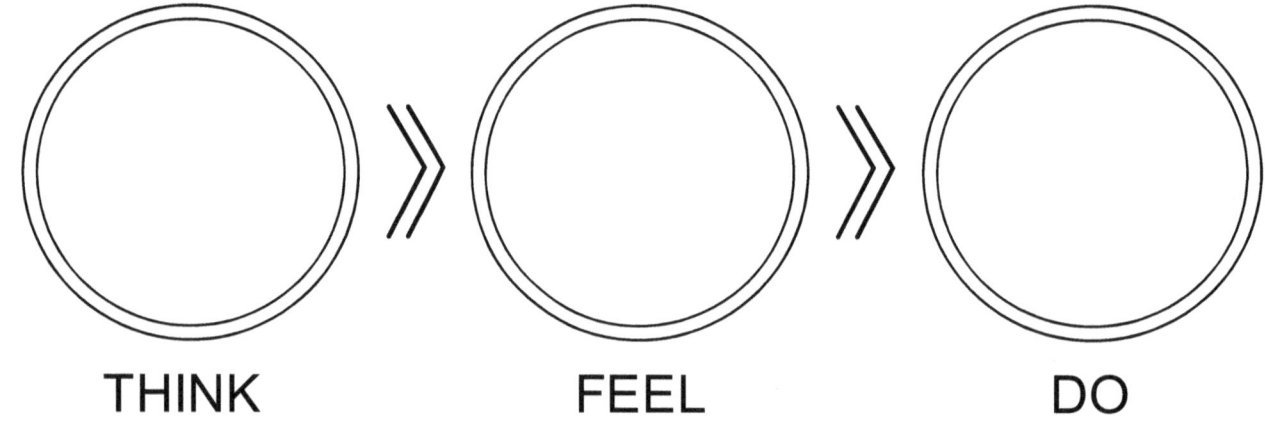

THINK   FEEL   DO

Look at the DO circle. Is that behavior helping you achieve your goal?

IF NOT, continue this activity to find a more satisfying, successful, constructive pattern. Remember that others don't make you think, feel or act in a certain way. You make those choices, even though you may not be aware you are doing that. Others can trigger your pattern, but it's your pattern. The changes come from creating a new pattern rather than looking for blame. Because you created the first pattern, you can create a different pattern, which will help you move closer to your goal.

You can create this new pattern by changing what you think, what you feel or what you do. You can decide, "How would I like to feel?" (Remember, words such as "like" and "that" are NOT feeling words, so use the Feeling Words if you need help identifying a feeling.)
Fill in the FEEL circle with the new feeling

OR you can decide, "What would I like to do different?" Fill this in the DO circle.
OR You can decide, "What would I rather tell myself?" Fill that in the THINK
circle. Use the affirmations on the next page if you need help.

When you filled in the one of the circles, you can work forward or backward to fill in the other two circles. For example, let's say you've decided that you would rather feel confident. You've written this in the FEEL circle. Now ask yourself "What would I have to tell myself to feel that way?" Write what you'd tell yourself in the THINKcircle.

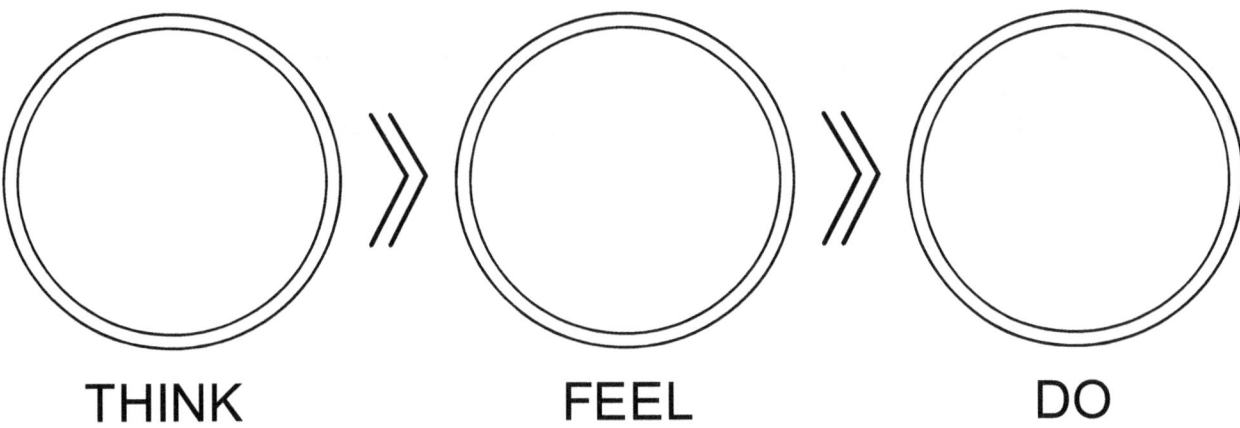

THINK   **FEEL**   **DO**

Now that you know what you want to feel and what you'd have to tell yourself to feel that way, you can decide what you would do. Ask yourself, "What would I do if I felt that way?" This becomes your DO circle.

You'll soon see how your thoughts influence your feelings and what you then do.

You can learn more about what is possible for you to do by creating a whole new series of decisions about what you think, feel and do for yourself.

Affirmations/ New thoughts:

I'm one of a kind, unique and special, and there will never be another just like
me, so there's no need to compare or compete.
I'm worthy just because I exist.
I love and approve of myself.
I deserve to be happy.
I'm 100 % responsible for what happens to me.
It's okay to make mistakes.
I can love, not scold, the child inside of me.
I trust myself.
I'm going to do things right now to be happy.
I'm lovable just as I am.

SELF - ESTEEM SUMMARY WORKSHEET

In this activity I learned:

Awareness — I'm a person who thinks_____, feels_____ and does_____
(Fill in with your first pattern.)

Acceptance — Without judgment I can remind myself that I can change any one of the circles and it will lead to changing all of the circles. I can tell myself, "It's okay for me to think, feel or do any of these things. That's just going on for me now."

Action — With courage to do homework in the real world, I can change my feeling to_____
_____
_____

or my thought to _____
_____
_____

or my action to _____
_____
_____

CHAPTER 12

SETTING GOALS

When you make your own decisions about how you want to use your time, set your own goals and make choices for yourself, you feel more encouraged. Making your own decisions means being pro-active. In this activity you can learn to be more active in making your own decisions rather than reacting to the decisions of others or to what happens to be going on around you.

Here are some steps to help you think about your goals.

Activity:

1. Take some time to think about your life now. It may help to see what fills your time by drawing a picture of what you're doing by using a circle to fill in the percent of time you currently spend in a typical day. (You may want to use the list below to help you think of areas in your life.)

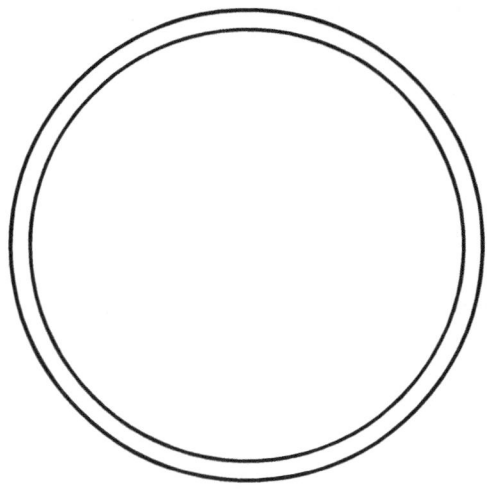

List: *work, kids, couple fun, family fun, vacations, exercise, health, household management, friends outside the family, extended family, spiritual growth, time for self.*

2. How would you like your life to be five years from now? (Think of how old you'll be or how old your children will be to help you get a clearer picture of what five years from now will mean.) List five things you'd like to see in your life.

1._____
2._____
3._____
4._____
5._____

THESE ARE YOUR LONG TERMGOALS.

3. Now ask yourself how you would like to spend life if you only had one month to live. List three things you'd do.

1._____
2._____
3._____

THESE ARE YOUR SHORT TERMGOALS.

4. Look at the lists in # 2 and #3. What jumps out at you? Are you doing anything in the present to achieve either your long term or short-term goals? Write out three conclusions you have after comparing these two lists.

Conclusion #1 _____
_____
_____

Conclusion #2 _____
_____
_____

Conclusion #3 _____
_____
_____

If you'd like to make some changes in your life so more of your goals are included but if you aren't certain how to proceed, there are some steps you can take to help you move in the direction you're heading. If a goal seems hard to reach, it sometimes helps to break the goal down into steps needed to reach it. Pick one of your goals and brainstorm ideas of things you could do to reach it.

GOAL:_____
_____

STEP #1:_____
_____
_____

STEP #2:_____
_____
_____

STEP #3:_____
_____
_____

NOW BREAK DOWN THE STEPS even further by picking one of the steps and breaking it down into MINI-STEPS. What are the first three things you'd have do for one of the Steps

STEP:_____
_____

MINI STEP #1:_____
_____

MINI STEP #2:_____
_____

MINI STEP #3:_____
_____

Now you can start by doing one of the MINI-STEPS to reach your goal.

SELF - ESTEEM SUMMARY WORKSHEET

In this activity I learned:

Awareness

I'm a person who has a long-term goal of _____
_____
(Fill in one of your long-term goals from the activity.)

Acceptance

Whout judgment, I can tell myself that it's okay if my goals and real day-today activities are the same or different. That's just what's happening in my life now. I can notice whether I'm
- Reactive?
- Proactive?
- Resistive to any activity that has the word goal or schedule in it?

Action

With courage to do homework in the real world, I can pick one of the ministeps from my list to begin. That mini-step is _____
_____

CHAPTER 13

UNDERSTANDING

Based on material from Jane Nelsen's book Understanding

Sometimes you can learn more about a reoccurring problem by increasing your understanding. When you do, it helps you let go of the things you can't control and use your strength and ideas to deal with the things you can control. This is called acceptance.

To move towards acceptance you need to realize there are many different realities. Every human being thinks his or her own thoughts, and everyone's thoughts are different. No one person's thoughts are better or worse, right or wrong. They are just different. Let's see how this works.

Activity:

1. What reoccurring problem would you like to work on?

_____
_____
_____
_____
_____
_____
_____
_____
_____
_____

2. What are your thoughts about this problem?

_____
_____
_____
_____
_____
_____
_____
_____
_____
_____

3. What do you think others' thoughts might be about this problem?

_____
_____
_____
_____
_____
_____
_____
_____
_____
_____

You may not have noticed or paid attention, but you probably have strong feelings happening inside of you when you think about this problem.

4. Think of the last time you were having this problem and go inside yourself to find out how you were feeling. Use only feeling words, not words such as I felt he, as if, they, etc. (Remember to use the Feeling Words on page 55 if you need help.)

I felt _____

Feelings are the best guide you have of what is really going on. Remember that feelings are inside of you and they give valuable information about you, not about others.

5. If you listen carefully to your feelings and let them guide you, where would they take you? What would you do?

_____
_____
_____
_____
_____
_____
_____
_____
_____

Life has cycles. Nothing lasts forever and what seems like a big deal today may be forgotten tomorrow.

6. If you thought about this problem as having a cycle, what would you tell yourself?

_____
_____
_____
_____
_____
_____
_____

SELF - ESTEEM SUMMARY WORKSHEET

In this activity I learned:

Awareness

I'm a person who sometimes feels _____

_____

_____

Acceptance

Whout judgment, I can tell myself, "These are my feelings. They're information about me and they're not good or bad, right or wrong. I can also remember that other people have different realities."

Action

With courage to do homework in the real world, I can choose one of the following: (Circle the number of the one you decide to do.)

1. I can ask others what their thoughts are instead of guessing.

2. I can give myself permission to listen to my feelings and trust them to guide me.

3. I can have faith in the process of life's cycles.

To know you is to

love yourself.

Courage comes from awareness

of who you are

and acceptance of who you are

(REMEMBER, YOU'RE GOOD ENOUGH

JUST AS YOU ARE.)

and taking action in the real world.

With courage, there is effort,

practice, learning, trying, doing

and growing.

So,

keep up the good work!

Have faith in yourself!

Do it!

Revised 4th edition

USE THIS BOOK TO LEARN ABOUT

*How to become aware of yourself in ways you never have

*How your inner child may be calling the shots of your adult relationships

*How your early decisions may be causing you reoccurring problems in your daily life

*How to re-parent your inner child

*How to practice self-acceptance and how to create small action steps for change

*How to apply Adlerian psychology and Positive Discipline to learn and grow

*USE THIS BOOK IN CONJUNCTION WITH DO IT YOURSELF THERAPY (Lynn Lott and Barbara Mendenhall) to become an Encouragement Consultant to yourself and others.

FOR PARENTS, COUNSELORS, COACHES, TEACHERS, ENCOURAGEMENT CONSULTANTS AND YOU

Marilyn Matulich Kentz attended the Family Education Center in Petaluma, CA. Her now grown children were little feisty tykes at the time and she knew she needed education and support. It was there that she met mentor, Lynn Lott, and was introduced to Adlerian Psychology. After joining weekly classes for several years, and after experiencing how well the practice of Positive Discipline worked on her own children, she began studying the philosophies of Alfred Adler and Rudolph Dreikurs. She coauthored two books with Ms. Lott *To Know Me is to Love Me* - a workbook based on the Adlerian theories of building selfesteem and Family Work: *Whose Job Is It?* – a guide for parents to engage children in household chores. Before she could continue with her education, Hollywood called. With her attention elsewhere (Hollywood, TV and stage), it wasn't until 2000 that her background in Family Education came to the forefront. Since then, Kentz has held classes in Positive Discipline and coaches many parents privately.

Dru West is a licensed Marriage & Family Therapist in private practice for over 25 years in Petaluma, California. She is married and the mother of four grown children. She first learned the principals of Adlerian Psychology when her children were young through Lynn Lott's training program at the Family Education Center. These principles helped form a solid foundation for understanding self and others, which she continues to use in her professional work. West is currently active with a group trying to make changes about hormonal birth control and the safety information given to women by healthcare professionals and the FDA. West also co-authored the first edition of *To Know Me Is to Love Me* in 1990.

Lynn Lott, MMFT, MA, is the founder of the Encouragement Consultant Trainings and co-founder of the Positive Discipline Association and collaborative founder of Positive Discipline. Lynn has been teaching Adlerian psychology and Positive Discipline since 1968 and has been working in private practice for most of her career helping parents, couples and individuals. She is the author of 20 books, including many in the Positive Discipline series. Her courses are popular throughout the US and China where she holds trainings once a year. Her DVD trainings are now used in 59 countries.

www.ingramcontent.com/pod-product-compliance
Lightning Source LLC
LaVergne TN
LVHW061255060426
835507LV00020B/2323